RULING IN ANCIENT EGYPT

By Robin Twiddy

LIFE LONG AGO

BookLife
PUBLISHING

©2021
BookLife Publishing Ltd.
King's Lynn
Norfolk PE30 4LS

ISBN: 978-1-83927-468-8

Written by:
Robin Twiddy

Edited by:
Emilie Dufresne

Designed by:
Danielle Webster-Jones

All rights reserved.
Printed in Malta.

A catalogue record for this book is available from the British Library.

All facts, statistics, web addresses and URLs in this book were verified as valid and accurate at time of writing. No responsibility for any changes to external websites or references can be accepted by either the author or publisher.

IMAGE CREDITS

Cover & throughout - Anna Panova, Ingotr, asantosg, artform, Panda Vector, Macrovecto, GoodStudio, Constantin Seltea. 4-5 aliaksei kruhlenia, Inspiring, ONYXprj. 9 - whanwhan.ai, ASAG Studio, ID-EasyDoor, Vanatchanan, ilkayalptekin, Mastak A, GoodStudio. 15 - Siberian Art. 16 - klyaksun, NotionPic. 18 - SkyPics Studio. 19 - OlgaChernyak. 21 - Panda Vector, matrioshka, klyaksun, Macrovector. 22 - azar nasib. Images are courtesy of Shutterstock.com. With thanks to Getty Images, Thinkstock Photo and iStockphoto.

CONTENTS

Page 4   Welcome to Paradise
Page 6   Morning at the Palace
Page 8   Royal Food
Page 10   Attending Court
Page 12   The Word of Law
Page 14   Everyone in Their Place
Page 16   Visiting the Temple
Page 18   Fun by the Nile
Page 20   Valley of the Kings
Page 22   Time to Relax
Page 24   Glossary and Index

Words that look like THIS can be found in the glossary on page 24.

We believe that life in Egypt is perfect. In fact, it is so perfect that the <u>AFTERLIFE</u> is just like it is here in Egypt. You even get to carry on with the job you had here on Earth.

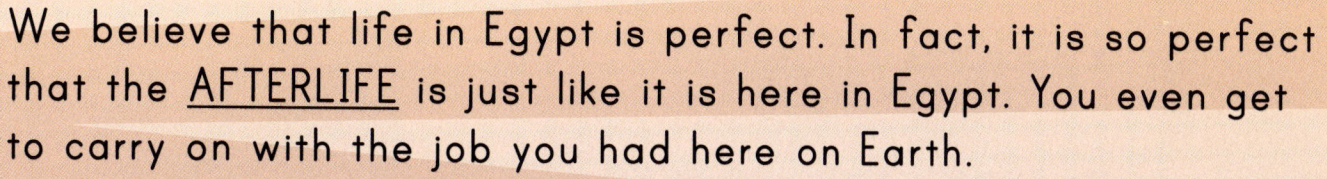

The gods placed my father, the Pharaoh, here to help guide his people.

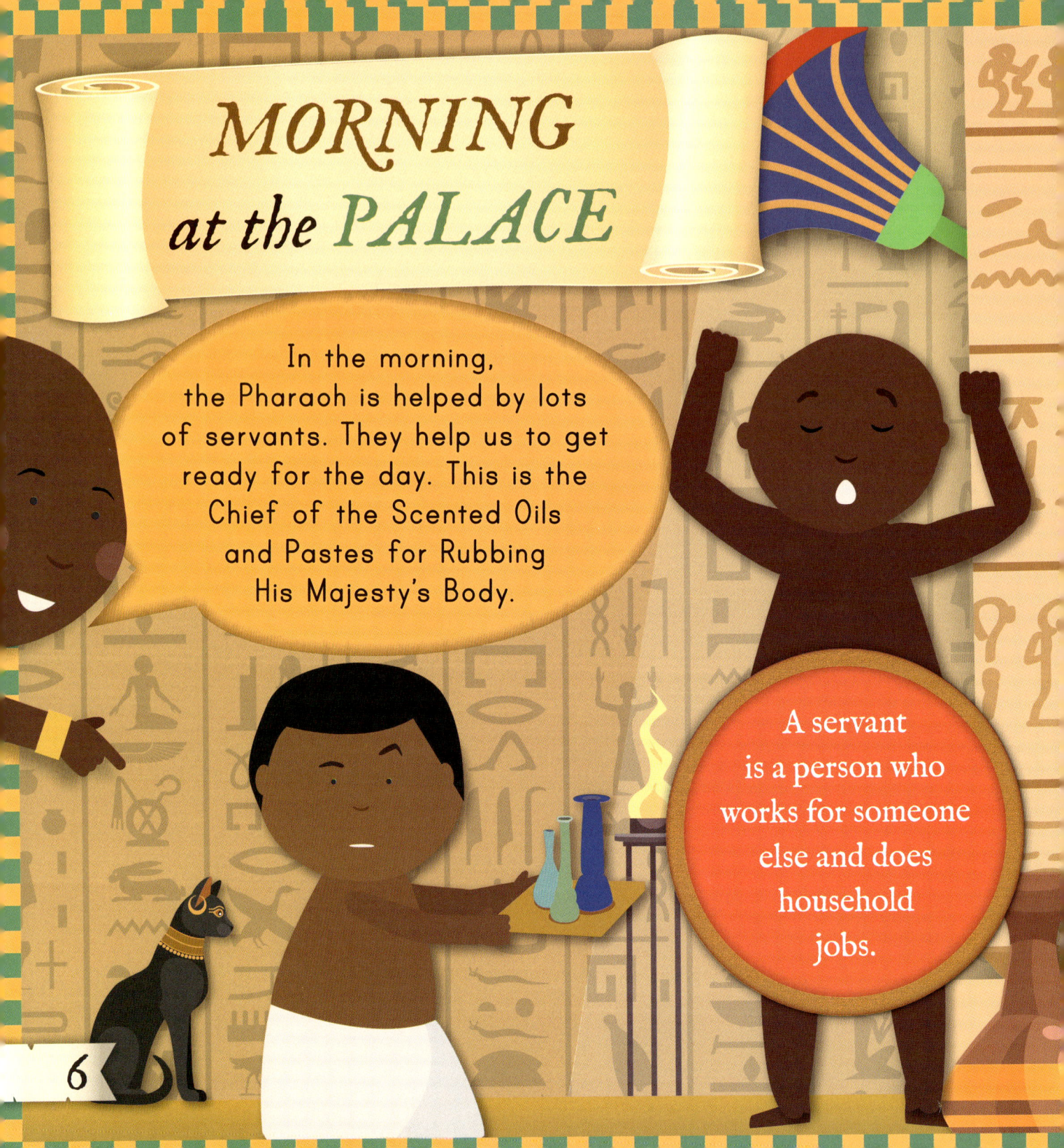

We eat all sorts of food in Egypt. Today's meal is duck. The poorer people only eat meat and <u>POULTRY</u> on special occasions. We can eat it every day because we are the royal family.

Bread
Onions
Beef
Dates
Fish

Like all pharaohs, my father is the highest power in all the land. That means he makes the LAWS. He will tell the court how to rule the country and they tell him news from all around Egypt.

Hi Pharaoh, we have set up a new TRADE route along the Nile.

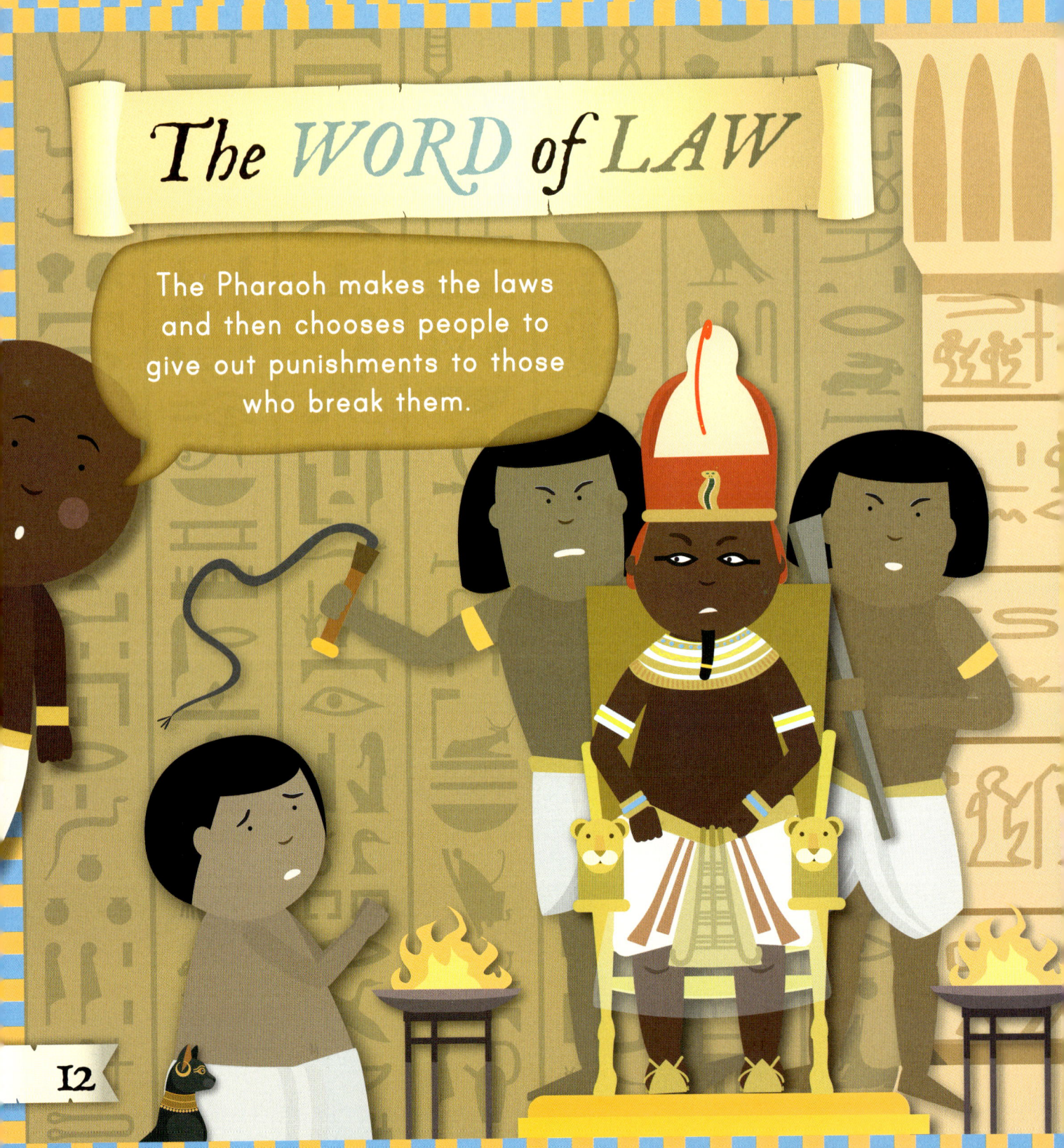

EVERYONE in Their PLACE

The gods placed the Pharaoh above everyone else. The nobles are below him and at the bottom are the <u>SLAVES</u> and servants. Everyone is happy with their place because that is what the gods want.

Look — it is a bit like a pyramid. Come on, I will show you.

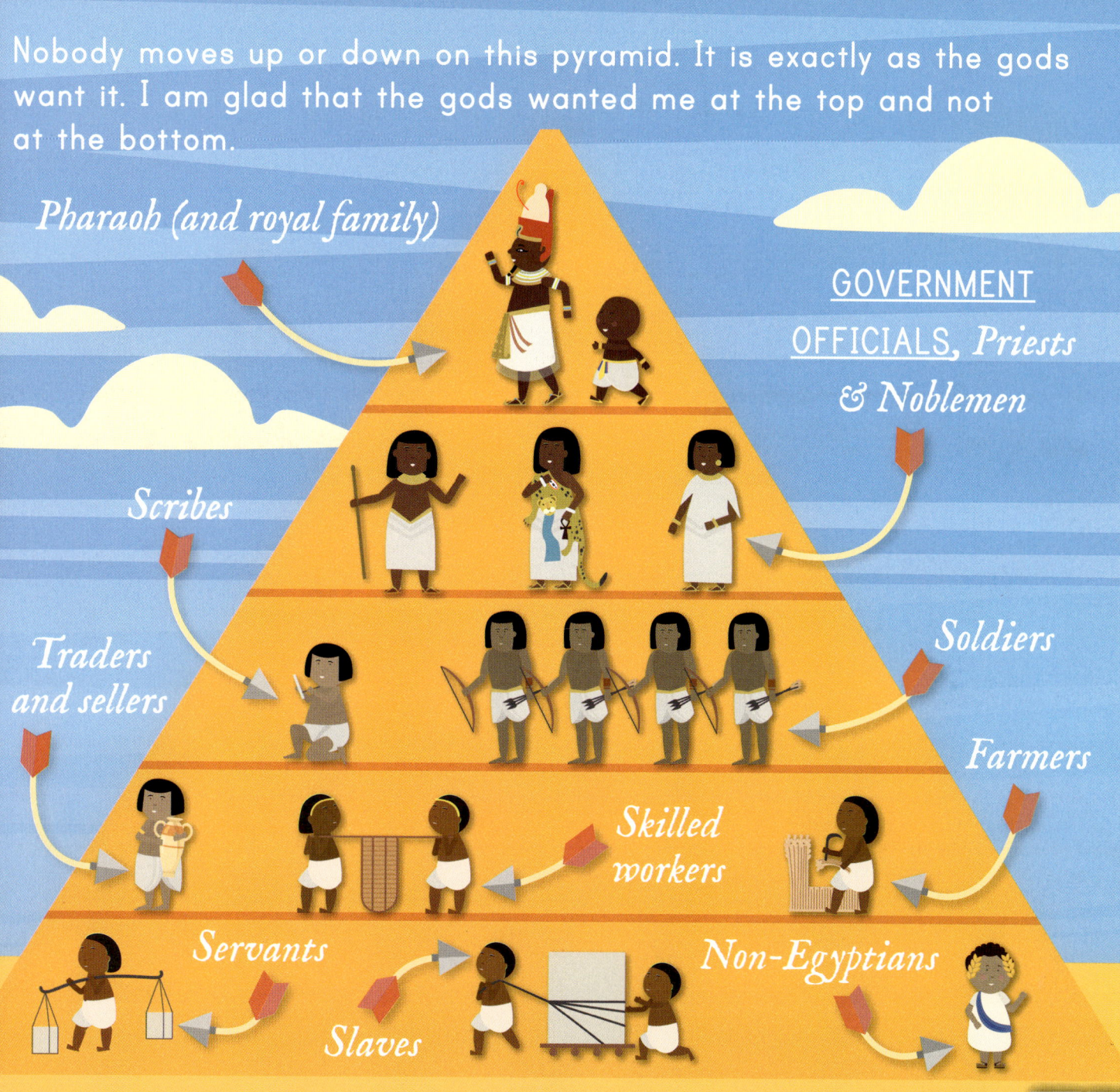

17

There are lots of fun activities in Egypt. Lots of people like to have swimming and boat races on the Nile, but I prefer playing senet with my friends.

Senet is one of the first board games ever invented.

VALLEY of the KINGS

My father is talking to his royal builder about his <u>TOMB</u> in the Valley of the Kings. When my father dies, he will be buried there with everything he needs for the afterlife.

The pharaohs of the New Kingdom hid their tombs underground in the Valley of the Kings so that robbers would not steal from them.

GLOSSARY

afterlife	life after death
enforce	make sure that something, such as a law, is met or carried out
government officials	people whose work involves helping to run a country
laws	the rules that a country or nation lives by
noblemen	people with a very high rank in a country
poultry	birds that are raised to be eaten
religious ceremonies	special activities that celebrate or are carried out for religious reasons
scribes	people whose job involves writing things down
slaves	people who are owned by another person and forced to work for them
tomb	a building or structure that houses dead bodies
trade	buying and selling
wisdom	having knowledge and being wise

INDEX

clothes 7
crowns 7
gods 5, 14–17, 23

hunting 18
laws 11–13
pharaohs 4–5, 11–15, 18, 20–21

senet 19
servants 6–7, 14–15, 18, 21
Vizier 13